SWING YOUR PARTNERS

A GUIDE TO
∽ MODERN COUNTRY DANCING ∾

by DURWARD MADDOCKS

Stephen Daye Press
Brattleboro, Vt.
$ 1.⁰⁰

THE PUBLISHER TO HIS READER

COUNTRY DANCING IS *FUN*, AND AMERICA IS FAST REDISCOVERING THIS FACT. IN APARTMENTS, DANCE HALLS, PRIVATE BALLROOMS AND COUNTRY GRANGES FROM COAST TO COAST, THESE DANCES ARE BRINGING GAIETY TO COUNTLESS GROUPS. WITH THE SPREAD OF THEIR POPULARITY HAS COME A NEED FOR A BOOK WHICH WOULD TEACH - NOT HOW THESE DANCES USED TO BE DONE OR ARE STILL DONE IN ANY SPECIFIC REGION OF THE UNITED STATES - BUT HOW THEY CAN BE DONE IN ANY AND EVERY REGION.

DURWARD MADDOCKS HAS WRITTEN, DESIGNED AND HAND-LETTERED JUST THIS SORT OF GUIDE. "SWING YOUR PARTNERS" WILL SERVE AS AN INSTRUCTION BOOK FOR BEGINNERS, A PROGRAM FOR THOSE WHO HAVE STUDIED IT AS A TEXT, AND A CALL-BOOK FOR THE EXPERIENCED OR NOVICE CALLER. THE AUTHOR HAS ILLUSTRATED IT WITH 500 OF HIS OWN SKETCHES AND DIAGRAMS WHICH DESCRIBE THE MEANING OF THE CALLS, THE FORMATIONS, AND THE PROCEDURE. HE HAS INCLUDED A DANCEABLE COLLECTION OF FIFTY OF THE SIMPLER SQUARE, CIRCLE AND CONTRA DANCES ... MOST OF THEM SQUARES, BECAUSE THESE ARE EASIER FOR THE BEGINNER TO LEARN AND MORE FUN FOR THOSE WHO LIKE CONSTANT ACTION. THE BOOK IS INGENIOUSLY CROSS-REFERENCED FOR ACTUAL USE ON THE DANCE FLOOR BY ANY GROUP OF BEGINNERS. AT THE SAME TIME, THE MORE EXPERIENCED WILL SEE WAYS TO MAKE AN INFINITE NUMBER OF DANCES FROM THOSE THAT APPEAR HERE. IN EITHER CASE, A PROFESSIONAL CALLER IS NOT REQUIRED. ANY DANCER WHO STUDIES THIS BOOK CAN HAVE THE FUN OF CALLING FOR HIS OWN GROUP.

THE AUTHOR is pioneering in a modern technique, which allows enough variation in both form and music so that any dancer may enjoy the dances in any locality. HE is not fighting the old timers, but helping the new timers. AFTER THE NEW TIMERS have mastered the fundamentals in this book, they will then be ready to dance with the old timers on their own ground.

THE COMBINATION of the Aligno binding and flexible backbone allows the caller or dancer to fold the book at any one page and hold it easily in the palm of his hand. ABOVE EVERYTHING, this book was created to simplify the process of learning the country dances. BY USING IT, any group of four or more couples with access to music, can entertain themselves ... gaily and in a genuinely social way.

STEPHEN DAYE PRESS

BRATTLEBORO, VERMONT

~ Table of Contents ~

Key to the Illustrations

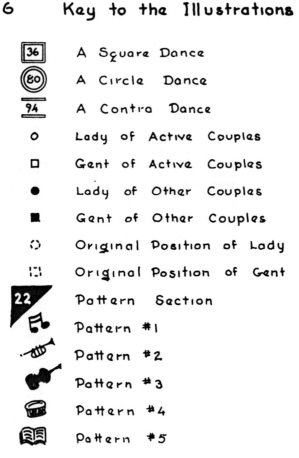

36	A Square Dance
80	A Circle Dance
94	A Contra Dance
o	Lady of Active Couples
□	Gent of Active Couples
●	Lady of Other Couples
■	Gent of Other Couples
◌	Original Position of Lady
⫶	Original Position of Gent
22	Pattern Section
	Pattern #1
	Pattern #2
	Pattern #3
	Pattern #4
	Pattern #5

The groups of dancers at the head of each "Dance-Page" show just how each set is formed.

This book was written for individuals and groups who want to do the square dances, for those who have never danced, for those who want to help others, and for those dancers who dare to be of real service to their fellow dancers by calling the changes for them.

This book contains only the simplest dances and calls, or changes. It is by no means a complete catalogue, but rather a danceable collection, written and illustrated for beginners, from the beginner's point of view.

Country dancing is as modern as we choose to make it today. We have the right to dance as we please, change steps if we want to. That is what gives this type of dancing vitality. The old timers stayed so close to the hard and fast lines of their dances that they could enjoy them only in their home towns. If the dancer today also wishes to become a purist in the country dances he may. But he must first know the fundamentals.

"Swing Your Partners" employs a new and simplified technique. This new technique allows enough variation and freedom so the dancers may enjoy the dances any where—from the hills of New England to the coast of California.

Many beginners are dismayed by the fancy quirks and variations in footwork which are used by the experts and old-timers in the country dances. The beginner will have plenty of time to introduce individual steps or shuffles after he has become thoroughly familiar with the meaning of the calls and the plan of the dances. The beginner will do better to _walk_ through the calls. Individual variations will develop later, naturally and without effort. Whatever these variations are, they should not interfere with the smooth progress of the set.

The term **SQUARE DANCING** is widely used when the general term **COUNTRY DANCING** is meant. Country dancing is made up of three types: **SQUARE,** such as "Birdie in the Cage"; **CIRCLE**, such as "Soldier's Joy" and **CONTRA,** such as "Lady of the Lake". The basic dance calls are the same for all three. The main difference is in the line-up, or formation.

THE SQUARE DANCE (pp. 13-79) is danced from a square formation by 4 couples, one couple to a side, each facing the center of the set. In this dance each person has a definite position and must always return to it at the end of the movement. A set of three square dances is called a **QUADRILLE.**

THE CIRCLE DANCE (pp 79-87) is danced from a large circle made up of small groups composed of 4, 6, or 8 people. After dancing a complete set of changes with the original group, each group proceeds around the circle, dancing with every other group in turn.

THE CONTRA DANCE (pp. 87-94) is danced from 2 contrary lines, with partners in opposite lines facing each other. In this dance every second couple works to the foot of the line, while the others work to the head. When those who started at the head have worked back to the head once more, the dance is finished.

In the Squares and Contras, as in the Circle dances, any number of sets may dance at the same time.

10 Music

The old timers had a special tune for each dance, but this led to confusion whenever they danced in a town where a different tune was played from the one to which they were accustomed. The modern technique allows the playing of any tunes or combinations of tunes for the same dance. People who learn under this flexible system can enjoy the dances in whatever part of the country they happen to be.

While all of the previously published books about country dancing have indicated the number of beats of music which should be allowed for each phase of the dance, this book purposely does not do this. If the beginner follows the music and the calls, his steps will almost automatically be completed in the right number of beats. Trying to remember the exact number will serve only to complicate his task.

For the squares and circles, the faster 2/4 or 4/4 tunes should be played, such as Soldier's Joy, Turkey in the Straw, polkas or any modern tune that can be played in 2/4 or 4/4 time.

For the contras, the slower 6/8 tunes should be played, such as Haste to the Wedding, Money Musk, most schottisches, or any modern tunes that can be played in 6/8 time.

Following is a list of music that can be used by a band for large groups, and a list of records for small groups. All of these have been tested on the dance floor.

*Just in time for insertion - Victor's square dance album "Swing Your Partner," also Columbia's album "Square Dances"

SHEET MUSIC

Seventy Good Old Dances;
      Oliver Ditson Co.   Boston

Old Familiar Dances;
      Oliver Ditson Co.   Boston

American Country Dances;
      G. Schirmer Inc,   New York

Dance Manual 61
      enclosed with "Good Morning" by H. Ford
      The Dearborn Publishing Co. Dearborn, Mich.

Pioneer Collection, Old Time Dances;
      Paull-Pioneer Music Co,   New York

RECORD LIST

Except where noted, records are for Squares & Circles.

DECCA

Turkey in the Straw, etc.	album 66	2647-A
Old Joe Clark, etc.		—— B
Fire in the Mountain, etc.	album 66	2648-A
Soldier's Joy, etc.		—— B
Sourwood Mountain, etc.	album 66	2649 A
Devil's Dream, etc.		—— B
Stone Rag		5393 A
College Hornpipe		—— B

SEARS

The Girl I Left Behind	7741
Turkey in the Straw	——

SEARS

Ragtime Annie Durang's Hornpipe	8738
Smokey Mountain Schottische (Contra) Kansas City Rag (with calls for caller)	8831

BLUEBIRD

Haste to the Wedding (Contra)	B-4976-A
Tanner's Rag Tanner's Hornpipe	B-5657-A ——— B
Straw Breakdown Florida Blues	B-6844-A ——— B

VICTOR

Medley of Old Time Reels Favorite Hornpipe Medley (Contra)	16393-A ——— B
Quadrille Figure #1 (slow enough for Contra) Quadrille Figure #2	20638-A ——— B
Quadrille Figure #3 Sicilian Circle	20639-A ——— B
Soldier's Joy Lady of the Lake (fast enough for square)	20592-A ——— B
Money Musk (Contra) Virginia Reels (traditional – perfect timing)	20447-A ——— B

THE SQUARE DANCE
This is the Procedure

In learning the square dance, first form the square and learn the names of the positions (p. 14). Then study the meaning of the calls (pp. 15-20). Practice each call until you know just what to do when that call is heard. In the process of learning the calls, and in order to know their relation to a complete square dance, turn to Pattern #1 (p. 22). This is one of the several patterns which square dances follow, and is a complete square dance in itself. Walk through each of the calls in the order in which they appear in the right-hand column until you see just how the "Dances" (pp. 35-67) are combined with the "Openings and Endings" (pp 32-33) to make a complete square dance.

When you have learned the names of the positions, the meaning of the calls, and the order of the #1 Pattern square dance, then choose any of the #1 Pattern dances in the book for further practice with music. You will then be ready to make full use of this book.

On each of the "Dances" (pp. 35-67) the note at the bottom of the page will show which of the several patterns to use in order to make a complete dance. It will then be obvious that you can combine different endings with different dances to make an infinite number of complete square dances.

In the Square Dance a set consists of four couples facing the center of a square. Each should be close enough to the other to be able to join hands without stretching. Each person has a definite place and that place is the one to which each <u>must</u> <u>always</u> <u>return</u>.

The names of the positions are: CALLER HERE

FIRST COUPLE or **HEAD COUPLE.** <u>The couple</u> <u>with its back to the caller is the first couple</u>, unless <u>told otherwise by the caller</u>.

SECOND COUPLE. The couple on the right of the first couple.

THIRD COUPLE. The couple opposite the first.

FOURTH COUPLE or **LAST COUPLE** The couple on the left of the first couple and opposite the second.

NEXT COUPLE. The couple next on the right.

TWO HEAD COUPLES, HEAD COUPLES, FIRST FOUR, HEAD FOUR, HEADS. The first and third couples are at times called by all these different names.

TWO SIDE COUPLES, SIDE COUPLES, SIDE FOUR, SIDES. The second and fourth couples are likewise known by these names.

CORNER or **CORNER PARTNER.** Your corner partner is the one with whom you form the corner of the imaginary square in which you dance. If you are a lady, your corner partner is the gent of the next couple to the right. If you are a gent your corner is the lady of the next couple to the left.

The call (or change) is the direction given
to the dancers by the person known as the
caller. If you learn what each of these calls
means, it is not necessary to know the whole
routine of any dance when it is named. The
caller will put the dance together call by call,
and if you know the meaning and procedure
of each change you simply listen for the calls
and do them one by one as they are given. Most
calls are designed to take you back to your
original place. The following calls are
danced in all country dancing (unless otherwise noted).

Note: In studying these calls, remember that
the lady is always at the right of the gent who is
her partner. And, except where noted, the steps
which are described in the explanations are
meant to be done by both the ladies and gents
at the same time.

SALUTE or HONOR or ADDRESS
Means to bow.

BALANCE
Both point right toe and then left
toe. Old timers substituted a tap or a
clog for the pointing

TURN WITH THE RIGHT HAND
Holding right hands, circle around
each other once, back to place.

TURN WITH THE LEFT HAND

 Holding left hands, circle around
each other once, back to position.

ALLEMANDE LEFT

 This is "Turn with the Left Hand", done
with your corner partner.

DO SI DO (dough see dough- Meaning Dos à Dos - back to back)

Face the person to whom the call is
directed, (say, Corner) both walk forward,
brush right shoulders together.
 Brush past each other back to back
by stepping over to the right.

Then brush left shoulders by walking
backward to place. You face in the same
direction throughout the steps.

The procedure is the same for any
number of people; singly, by twos,
fours, or in a line. You go around
only the one person you are facing.
DoSiDo should not be confused with
the western version which is a variety
of Right and Left, and Ladies Chain
combined.

PROMENADE

 Each person puts an arm behind the
other. Both walk around the circle <u>to the</u>
<u>right</u> back to their places. When the call is
HALF PROMENADE walk only to the
opposite side (that is, half way around).

Take the couple-dance, or waltz position. Stand side to side facing in opposite directions, and with the outsides of the right feet touching. Now push off with the left foot. You really run around after each other while holding the regular dance position. Be sure to pick up the right foot every time so that the pivot point will be between the two of you. Keep the feet as near the pivot point as possible and the upper body out away, otherwise you will be swung completely off your feet.

RIGHT AND LEFT.

Two couples who face each other walk forward.

Each Lady passes between the opposite Lady and gent, and goes directly to the place where the opposite lady stood, while her partner walks by on the outside.

The gent then takes his partner's hand (only while learning) and backs around into the place where the opposite gent was originally standing.

The lady turns with him so that both are in the opposite couple's original position. (continued over)

18 | Each couple has now done a **HALF RIGHT AND LEFT** and each must complete the change by going through the same steps back to his original place.

RIGHT AND LEFT EIGHT

 This is the same as Right and Left except that it is done by two groups (as in 62) at the same time, side by side.

LADIES CHAIN

 Two couples face each other. The two ladies walk forward to the center, take right hands and both walk past each other.

 Both take their opposite gent's left hand,

 and walk around him.

Then both ladies advance to the center and the movement is repeated with their own partners to complete the change. The gents turn in their own places.

LADIES GRAND CHAIN (not danced in contra)

This is the same as Ladies Chain except that four ladies advance to the center, cross right hands and go around, give left hand to the opposite (same) gent as before, go around him, ladies cross right hands again, left hand to partner and around him.

GENTS GRAND CHAIN (not danced in contra)

This is the same as "Ladies Grand Chain" except that the four gents advance to the center.

When each takes the opposite lady's left hand to go around her she stands still and holds his hand over her head while he walks around her.

Sometimes the gent and lady just hook left elbows and both walk around.

In this call the gents do all the changing and the ladies stay in their places all the time.

GRAND RIGHT AND LEFT

Standing in the square dance set or a circle, take your partner by the right hand, both walk by. All the ladies go in one direction to the left and all the gents go in the other direction to the right.

Then take the next person by the left hand, next by the right, and so on, hand over hand around the circle. Go around only once and always stop when you return to your own place.

In HALF GRAND RIGHT AND LEFT you stop when you meet your partner on the other side.

FOUR HANDS AROUND or CIRCLE FOUR

Join hands and circle to the left. This call is the same for any number of people:

THREE — SIX — SEVEN — or EIGHT HANDS AROUND.

CROSS RIGHT HANDS AROUND or
RIGHT HANDS ACROSS or
STAR WITH THE RIGHT

 It is done by 4 people; sometimes it is 4 ladies, 4 gents or 2 couples. It starts out the same as "Ladies Grand Chain". Four advance to the center, take hold of opposite's (lady to lady, gent to gent) right hand and walk around once, then —

BACK WITH THE LEFT or
LEFT HANDS BACK

Change hands, put left hand into the center and walk back the other way to place.

FORWARD AND BACK

Means to walk forward to the center and back to place.

Note: When calls not listed above appear in dances throughout the book they are usually found only in that one dance and are explained as they occur.

This section is the clearing-house for the Square Dance. It shows what a Complete Dance is like, how it is called, and the way it is put together. It shows that the square dance follows a general pattern which allows everyone an equal amount of dancing. It shows how the "Opening and Ending" calls (p. 32) are combined with the basic dance-calls which are repeated for each couple or set of couples, to make a complete dance. _Three of these complete dances_ make a Quadrille, which is danced with the same partner as a set of three dances is in ball-room dancing.

The plain and regular square patterns should be mastered in every particular before any variations are tried.

The symbol (such as a fiddle) at the head of each pattern-page, corresponds with the symbol of a "dance" (pp. 35-78) of the same pattern. This device will serve as a quick reference for the caller who wants to give variety to the program he puts together.

♫ PATTERN #1 ♫

This type of dance is danced by the head couples and then by the side couples. The first couple dances only with the third couple and the second couple dances only with the fourth. This example is "Round the Town" page 40. Any dance with the ♫ symbol may be substituted.

PATTERN

An Opening

The Dance

An Ending

EXAMPLE

ALL - EIGHT HANDS AROUND - (from page 32)

HEAD COUPLES
FOUR HANDS AROUND

HEAD COUPLES
RIGHT AND LEFT

HEAD COUPLES
FORWARD AND BACK

HEAD COUPLES
DO SI DO

ALL - SWING YOUR PARTNERS, PROMENADE.

The Dance

SIDE COUPLES
FOUR HANDS AROUND
SIDE COUPLES
RIGHT AND LEFT
SIDE COUPLES
FORWARD AND BACK
SIDE COUPLES
DO SI DO

An Ending *

ALL - SWING YOUR PARTNERS, PROMENADE

The Dance

HEAD COUPLES FOUR HANDS 'ROUND
SIDES FOUR HANDS 'ROUND
HEADS RIGHT AND LEFT
SIDES RIGHT AND LEFT
HEADS FORWARD AND BACK
SIDES FORWARD AND BACK
HEADS DO SI DO
SIDES DO SI DO

An Ending *

ALL - SWING YOUR PARTNERS, PROMENADE.

* Extra Endings may be added at the end and middle of the dance."

🎺 PATTERN # 2 🎺

In this type of dance, the whole routine is called once for each couple (or lady or gent, whichever is specified in the dance). That is, couple 1 dances with couples 2, 3, and 4; couple 2 dances with couples 3, 4, and 1; then couple 3 dances with couples 4, 1, and 2; and couple 4 dances with couples 1, 2, and 3. This example is "Life goes to a Party" page 39.

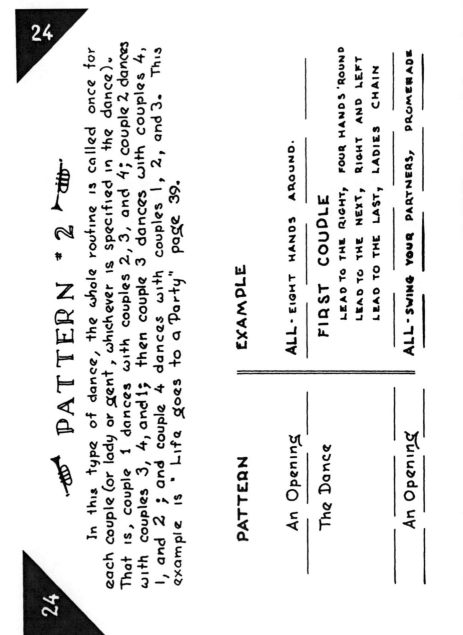

PATTERN | **EXAMPLE**

An Opening | ALL· EIGHT HANDS AROUND.

The Dance | FIRST COUDLE
 | LEAD TO THE RIGHT, FOUR HANDS 'ROUND
 | LEAD TO THE NEXT, RIGHT AND LEFT
 | LEAD TO THE LAST, LADIES CHAIN

 | ALL· SWING YOUR PARTNERS, PROMERADE

An Opening |

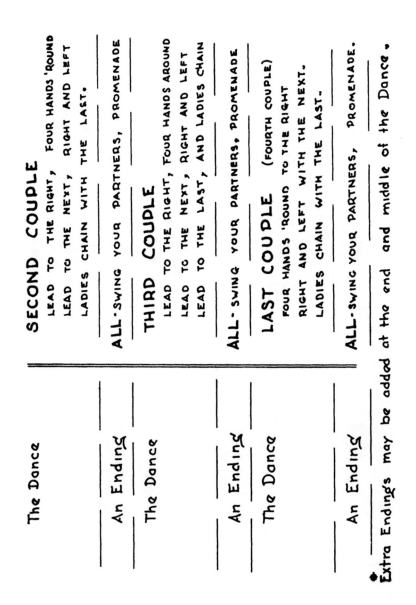

The Dance

SECOND COUPLE

LEAD TO THE RIGHT, FOUR HANDS 'ROUND
LEAD TO THE NEXT, RIGHT AND LEFT
LADIES CHAIN WITH THE LAST.

ALL · SWING YOUR PARTNERS, PROMENADE

THIRD COUPLE

LEAD TO THE RIGHT, FOUR HANDS AROUND
LEAD TO THE NEXT, RIGHT AND LEFT
LEAD TO THE LAST, AND LADIES CHAIN

ALL · SWING YOUR PARTNERS, PROMENADE

LAST COUPLE (FOURTH COUPLE)

FOUR HANDS 'ROUND TO THE RIGHT
RIGHT AND LEFT WITH THE NEXT.
LADIES CHAIN WITH THE LAST.

ALL · SWING YOUR PARTNERS, PROMENADE.

An Ending

The Dance

An Ending

The Dance

An Ending

♣ Extra Endings may be added at the end and middle of the Dance.

PATTERN #3

Here, the dance calls are called three times for each couple.[1]

An Opening
The Dance

ALL - EIGHT HANDS AROUND.
1st. LEAD TO THE RIGHT, BALANCE THE OLD MAN
(gent) SWING THE OLD MAN'S DAUGHTER.
RUN AWAY HOME AND SWING YOUR OWN.
↳ LEAD TO THE NEXT, BALANCE THE OLD MAN
SWING THE OLD MAN'S DAUGHTER.
RUN AWAY HOME AND SWING YOUR OWN.
↳ LEAD TO THE LAST, BALANCE THE OLD MAN
SWING THE OLD MAN'S DAUGHTER.
RUN AWAY HOME AND SWING YOUR OWN.

An Ending
The Dance

ALL-SWING YOUR PARTNERS, PROMENADE
2nd. LEAD TO THE RIGHT, BALANCE THE OLD MAN
(gent) SWING THE OLD MAN'S DAUGHTER
RUN AWAY HOME AND SWING YOUR OWN
↳ LEAD TO THE NEXT, BALANCE THE OLD MAN
SWING THE OLD MAN'S DAUGHTER
RUN AWAY HOME AND SWING YOUR OWN
↳ LEAD TO THE LAST, BALANCE THE OLD MAN
SWING THE OLD MAN'S DAUGHTER.
RUN AWAY HOME AND SWING YOUR OWN

The Dance

The Dance

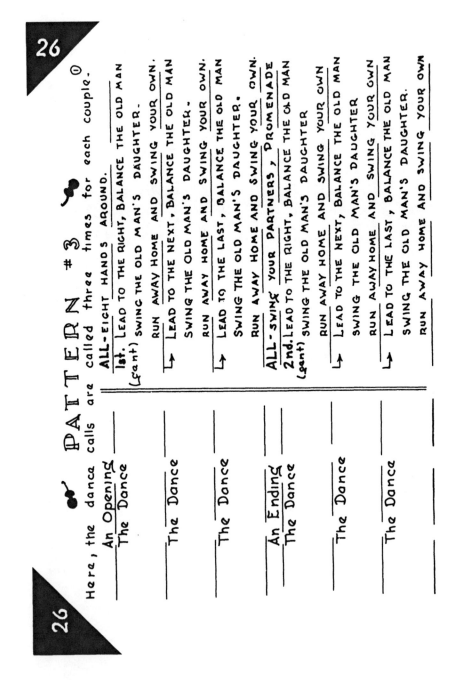

An Ending *
The Dance

ALL SWING YOUR PARTNERS, PROMENADE.
3rd. LEAD TO THE RIGHT, BALANCE THE OLD MAN
(gent) SWING THE OLD MAN'S DAUGHTER.

The Dance

↳ RUN AWAY HOME, SWING YOUR OWN.
↳ LEAD TO THE NEXT, BALANCE THE OLD MAN
SWING THE OLD MAN'S DAUGHTER.

The Dance

RUN AWAY HOME, SWING YOUR OWN.
↳ LEAD TO THE LAST, BALANCE THE OLD MAN
SWING THE OLD MAN'S DAUGHTER.

An Ending
The Dance

RUN AWAY HOME, SWING YOUR OWN.
ALL SWING YOUR PARTNERS, PROMENADE.
4th. LEAD TO THE RIGHT, BALANCE THE OLD MAN
(gent) SWING THE OLD MAN'S DAUGHTER

The Dance

↳ RUN AWAY HOME, SWING YOUR OWN
↳ LEAD TO THE NEXT, BALANCE THE OLD MAN
SWING THE OLD MAN'S DAUGHTER

The Dance

RUN AWAY HOME, SWING YOUR OWN
↳ LEAD TO THE LAST, BALANCE THE OLD MAN
SWING THE OLD MAN'S DAUGHTER

An Ending *

RUN AWAY HOME, SWING YOUR OWN.
SWING YOUR PARTNERS, PROMENADE

* Extra Endings may be added at the end and middle of the Dance.
⊙ couple, or lady, or gent whichever the dance species.

❂ PATTERN #4 ❂

In this type of dance the same routine of changes is done twice. First, it is danced by the head couples, head ladies, or head Gents, (whichever the dance calls for). When the routine is repeated, the side couples, side ladies or side Gents dance the same set of calls which the heads have previously danced. This is different from Pattern #1 only in that the calls cannot be alternated between Heads and Sides as they are in the last part of Pattern #1.

PATTERN

An Opening

EXAMPLE

ALL SWING YOUR PARTNERS AND ALL PROMENADE.

The Dance

2 HEAD LADIES

TURN YOUR RIGHT HAND GENT
WITH YOUR RIGHT HAND 'ROUND
TURN OPPOSITE WITH THE LEFT
SWING YOUR PARTNER IN THE CENTER
AND FOUR HANDS 'ROUND.

An Ending *

ALL—DO SI DO WITH YOUR CORNERS ALL
AND DO THE SAME WITH YOUR OWN LITTLE DOLL
RIGHT HAND TO YOUR PARTNERS
AND GRAND RIGHT AND LEFT.

The Dance

2 SIDE LADIES

TURN YOUR RIGHT HAND GENT
WITH YOUR RIGHT HAND 'ROUND
TURN OPPOSITE WITH THE LEFT
SWING YOUR PARTNER IN THE CENTER
AND FOUR HANDS 'ROUND.

An Ending *

ALL JOIN HANDS AND FORWARD ALL
AND SWING THE GAL ACROSS THE HALL (OPP)
NOW RUN AWAY HOME AND SWING YOUR OWN
AND ALL PROMENADE.

*Extra endings may be added at the middle and end of the dance

📖 PATTERN #5 📖

In this pattern the dance is called for either the four ladies or the four Gents, whichever the dance specifies. The routine is repeated four times. At the end of the fourth time each dancer is necessarily back in his original position. As some of "the Dances" are quite short they can be completely repeated if desired.
① Note: When there is rhyming, "The Ending" is included in "The Dance."

PATTERN

An Opening

The Dance

EXAMPLE

ALL DO SI DO WITH YOUR CORNER
DO SI DO WITH YOUR PARTNER
RIGHT HAND TO YOUR PARTNER
GRAND RIGHT AND LEFT.

FOUR GENTS TO THE RIGHT OF THE RING
WHEN YOU GET THERE
YOU BALANCE AND SWING

WHEN YOU GET THROUGH REMEMBER THE CALL
ALLEMANDE LEFT AND PROMENADE ALL.

— (Ending) ⊙ —

The Dance

FOUR GENTS TO THE RIGHT OF THE RING
WHEN YOU GET THERE
YOU BALANCE AND SWING
WHEN YOU GET THROUGH REMEMBER THE CALL
ALLEMANDE LEFT AND PROMENADE ALL

— (Ending) ⊙* —

The Dance

FOUR GENTS TO THE RIGHT OF THE RING-
WHEN YOU GET THERE
YOU BALANCE AND SWING.
WHEN YOU GET THROUGH REMEMBER THE CALL
ALLEMANDE LEFT AND PROMENADE ALL.

— (Ending) ⊙ —

The Dance

FOUR GENTS TO THE RIGHT OF THE RING-
WHEN . YOU GET THERE
YOU BALANCE AND SWING.
WHEN YOU GET THROUGH REMEMBER THE CALL.
ALLEMANDE LEFT AND PROMENADE ALL.

— (Ending) ⊙* —

*Extra Endings may be added at the middle and end of the dance.

These are movements that are danced by everyone together in contrast to the "Dance" which is done only by individuals or couples. These movements may be interchanged or subsituted for each other at will, and used for either openings or endings. Two or three can be joined together, and parts from each may be dropped to form different and interesting changes. As the dancers become more expert, the caller may make up combinations. The opening and ending calls are to be combined with an individual dance chosen from "the Dance" section as shown in the different "Patterns" to make a complete square dance.

In the following sections the capital letters comprise the minimum spoken call; the small letters are the rhymings, or the under-stood calls which are called for the beginners so that they will not hesitate; and the material in parentheses ( ) is explanation or information about the call, and not the call itself.

EIGHT HANDS AROUND

ALL SWING your **PARTNERS** and all **PROMENADE.**

(continued on next page)

THE OTHER WAY back you are _going wrong._

RIGHT HAND TO your PARTNERS all
GRAND RIGHT AND LEFT around the hall.

DO SI DO with YOUR CORNER
DO SI DO with YOUR PARTNER
RIGHT HAND TO your PARTNER
GRAND RIGHT AND LEFT.

CROSS RIGHT HANDS AROUND
LEFT HANDS BACK
SWING YOUR PARTNERS
AND PROMENADE

LADIES GRAND CHAIN
all PROMENADE

ALLEMANDE LEFT with your corners all
GRAND RIGHT AND LEFT around the hall

ALL JOIN HANDS and forward all
SWING THE GAL across the hall (opposite)
now run away home and SWING YOUR OWN
ALL PROMENADE.

34 ● Notes ●

The dances in the 'following section are the parts of the square dances which are different in each case. "The Dance" is the part which is danced by individuals, couples or groups in contrast to the "Openings and Endings" which are danced by everyone together in the set. They must be used in conjunction with the "Openings and Endings" as illustrated in the "Patterns" to form a complete dance.

Because many of the old dances were just called "Figures" each dance in this book has been given a name, for easy reference by dancer and caller.

The dances in this section are so arranged that any 3 complete dances in a row, used according to its "Pattern", will make a danceable quadrille. Just start with any dance and turn to the following two.

In the following dances the capital letters comprise the minimum spoken call; the small letters are the rhymings, or the understood calls, which are called for the beginners so that they will not hesitate; and the material in parentheses ( ) is explanation of information about the call, and not the call itself.

SIMPLE SIMON

| 36 | HEAD COUPLES
start the dance |

 FORWARD AND BACK

LADIES CHAIN

  FOUR HANDS 'ROUND

RIGHT AND LEFT.

Combine these calls with calls from page 32 as outlined on page 22 to make a complete dance.

LADIES & GENTS FAVORITE

 HEAD COUPLES
start the dance

37

FORWARD AND BACK ——→

FORWARD AGAIN
FIRST LADY CROSS OVER
(gent in between the two ladies)

FORWARD THREE AND BACK

FORWARD AGAIN
LADIES CROSS TO OTHER GENT

FORWARD THREE AND BACK

FORWARD AGAIN
FOUR HANDS HALF AROUND
HALF RIGHT AND LEFT
TO PLACE

See page 28 to make a Complete Dance.

OLD MAN'S DAUGHTER

38

FIRST GENT
starts the dance

 LEAD TO THE RIGHT
BALANCE to THE OLD MAN (the gent)

SWING THE OLD MAN'S
DAUGHTER (the lady)

 Now run away home and
SWING YOUR OWN
let the old man swing his daughter.

LEAD TO THE NEXT (etc.)

This same dance for the ladies is called
OLD ARKANSAW First Lady starts
LEAD TO THE RIGHT
 SWING YER MAW (elbow whirl)
SWING YER PAW
NOW DON'T FORGET
OLD ARKANSAW (your own)
See page 26 to make a Complete Dance.

LIFE GOES TO A PARTY

FIRST COUPLE
starts the dance.

39

LEAD TO THE RIGHT
FOUR HANDS AROUND

 LEAD TO THE NEXT
RIGHT AND LEFT

LEAD TO THE LAST
LADIES CHAIN

Combine these calls with calls
from page 32 as outlined on page 24
to make a complete dance.

'ROUND THE TOWN

40 HEAD COUPLES
start the dance.

FOUR HANDS 'ROUND
(once)

 RIGHT AND LEFT

FORWARD AND BACK

DO SI DO

Combine these calls with calls
from page 32 as outlined on page 22
to make a Complete Dance.

MERRY GO 'ROUND

FIRST GENT
starts the Dance.

41

TURN RIGHT HAND LADY
(this is the second lady)
WITH RIGHT HAND 'ROUND

turn **LEFT HAND LADY**
(this is the fourth lady)
WITH LEFT HAND 'ROUND

turn **OPPOSITE LADY**
(this is the third lady)
WITH BOTH HANDS 'ROUND

turn **PARTNER IN THE CENTER**
and **SIX HANDS 'ROUND**
on the merry go 'round.

NOTE: This dance can also be called for the ladies, by changing the words LADY to GENT.

See page 24 to make a Complete Dance.

LADY 'ROUND THE LADY

42 FIRST COUPLE
starts the Dance

LEAD TO THE RIGHT
go between the two

LADY 'ROUND THE LADY
GENT 'ROUND THE GENT

LADY 'ROUND THE GENT
GENT 'ROUND THE LADY

CIRCLE FOUR

LEAD TO THE NEXT (etc.)

Combine these calls with calls
from page 32 as outlined on page 26
to make a complete dance.

THE CUT-OFF

FIRST COUPLE
starts the dance.

SWING IN THE CENTER
AND DON'T GET MIXED

DOWN THE CENTER AND
CUT OFF SIX. ⟶

SWING IN THE CENTER
AS YOU DID BEFORE

DOWN THE CENTER AND
CUT OFF FOUR ⟶

SWING IN THE CENTER
AS YOU USED TO DO

DOWN THE CENTER AND
CUT OFF TWO ⟶

43

Combine these calls with calls
from page 32 as outlined on page 24
to make a Complete Dance

THE CALEDONIANS

44

AN OPENING   (page 32)

 FOUR LADIES
TO THE RIGHT and SWING the GENTS

FOUR GENTS
TO THE LEFT and SWING the LADIES

FOUR LADIES
TO THE RIGHT and SWING the GENTS

FOUR GENTS
TO THE LEFT and SWING the LADIES

AN ENDING   (page 32)

A note to the caller :-
If the dancers <u>can take it</u>, repeat the above
after an ending so they can get back to their
places.   If they look tired, let them Promenade
<u>half</u> around to their original places.

This is a good dance with which to end
the evening. The dancers must be very
careful to stay at the place to which they
advance until ready to advance again.
This is a Complete Dance, but can be repeated.

DOUBLE CROSS

 HEAD COUPLES
start the Dance

45

FORWARD AND BACK

 CROSS RIGHT HANDS AROUND
LEFT HAND BACK →

DO SI DO FOUR

LADIES CHAIN

Combine these calls with calls
from page 32 as outlined on page 22
to make a complete dance.

THE BEACHCOMBER

46 FIRST COUPLE
starts the Dance

 LEAD TO THE RIGHT
FOUR HANDS AROUND

 LEAD TO THE NEXT
SIX HANDS AROUND

LEAD TO THE LAST
EIGHT HANDS AROUND

Note: **CIRCLE SIX**, the gent
of the first couple and the lady of the other
couple drop hands and include the third
couple. **CIRCLE EIGHT**, first gent breaks
the circle and includes the last couple.
LEAD TO THE NEXT should be called just
as the first gent is circling into the center
so that he may continue on without a
pause and include the next couple.
See page 24 to make a Complete Dance.

TAKE A PEEK

 FIRST COUPLE
starts the Dance

 **LEAD TO THE RIGHT
go BEHIND THAT COUPLE
and TAKE A PEEK!**

 **BACK IN THE CENTER
and SWING SO NEAT.**

**BEHIND THAT COUPLE
PEEK ONCE MORE**

 **BACK IN THE CENTER
CIRCLE FOUR.**

LEAD TO THE NEXT (etc.)

Note: It is fun to say **YOU-HOO**
when you peek at each other **BEHIND
THAT COUPLE.**

See page 26 to make a Complete Dance.

BRING 'EM BACK ALIVE

48

 ALL FORWARD AND BACK

HEADS LADIES CHAIN

 SIDES RIGHT AND LEFT

  ALL FOUR GENTS
CROSS RIGHT HANDS 'ROUND
BRING opposite LADY BACK
BRING EM BACK ALIVE
(with a promenade)

Combine these calls with calls
from page 32 as outlined on page 28
to make a Complete Dance.

NICK AND CUT

FIRST COUPLE
starts the dance

49

 LEAD TO THE RIGHT
BEHIND THAT COUPLE
LADY GOES 'ROUND BUT NOT THE GENT

NICK EM WITH A BALANCE
(lady in center, gent on outside.)

 SPIN around and
(turn around individually in place.)

CUT EM RIGHT IN TWO
SWING IN THE CENTER

LADIES CHAIN
(lead to the next)

    This dance is a good example of how original dances may be made. It is built around the names of Nichols and Cutler in whose honor it was created.

See page 26 to make a Complete Dance.

POSTMAN'S HOLIDAY

50

GENTS   TO THE CENTER and
COME RIGHT BACK

LADIES   TO THE CENTER
STAND BACK TO BACK

ALL FOUR GENTS
TO THE RIGHT OF THE RING
GO ONCE AND A QUARTER
AND NOW ALL SWING

NOTE: In this dance it is the gents
who leave their places and move around.
The ladies always return to the same place.
See page 30 to make a complete dance.

JAMBOREE

HEAD COUPLES
start the dance

51

FORWARD   AND   BACK

 RIGHT   AND   LEFT

LADIES   CHAIN

 RIGHT   HANDS   ACROSS
LEFT   HANDS   BACK

FOUR   HANDS   'ROUND
SWING   YOUR   OPPOSITE

ALL   SWING   YOUR   OWN

Combine   these   calls   with   calls
from pages 32 as outlined   on   page 22
to make a Complete Dance.

BLUEBEARD

52

FIRST GENT
starts the dance

LEAD TO THE RIGHT, CIRCLE THREE
SWING LADY AND TAKE HER HOME
CIRCLE THREE IN THE CENTER.

LEAD TO THE NEXT, CIRCLE THREE
SWING LADY AND TAKE HER HOME
CIRCLE FOUR IN THE CENTER.

LEAD TO THE LAST, CIRCLE THREE
SWING LADY AND TAKE HER HOME
CIRCLE FOUR, BLUE BEARD IN THE CENTER.
(or Four Hands around The Blue Beard #1)

ALL FORWARD and
SWING YOUR OWN.

Each gent in turn becomes the
BLUE BEARD and then proceeds to collect
his quota of wives.
See page 24 to make a Complete Dance.

LADY FOR A DAY

FIRST LADY
starts the dance

 **TURN RIGHT HAND GENT
WITH RIGHT HAND 'ROUND**

TURN THE NEXT gent
WITH THE LEFT hand 'round

 turn **THE LAST** gent,
WITH THE RIGHT hand 'round

turn **PARTNER IN THE CENTER**
and **SIX HANDS AROUND**
that lovely couple.

In the above calls, the lady does a kind of GRAND RIGHT AND LEFT, only she walks completely around each gent, and ends by swinging her partner in the center.

See page 24 to make a Complete Dance.

DIP FOR THE OYSTER

54

FIRST COUPLE
starts the Dance

**LEAD TO THE RIGHT
FOUR HANDS 'ROUND**

DIP FOR THE OYSTER ──→ #1

DIG FOR THE CLAM #2

**DIVE FOR THE SARDINE
GET A FULL CAN.** #3

and **LEAD TO THE NEXT.** etc.

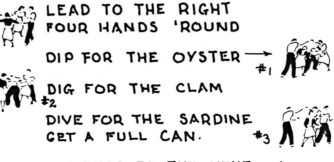

#1 While still holding hands, the first two duck under the raised arms of the second and back.

#2 The second two duck under the first and back out. #3. The first couple ducks under again, drops hands and continues on to the next.

See page 26 to make a Complete Dance.

TRAIL BLAZER

HEAD COUPLES
start the dance

55

FORWARD AND BACK

LADIES CHAIN

FORWARD AND DO SI DO.

RIGHT AND LEFT

FOUR HANDS 'ROUND

HALF RIGHT AND LEFT
HALF PROMENADE.

Combine these calls with calls from page 32 as outlined on page 22 to make a Complete Dance.

GOLDEN GATE

56 FIRST COUPLE starts the dance

 DOWN THE CENTER
THROUGH THE GOLDEN GATE

LADY GO RIGHT, GENT GO LEFT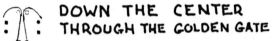
around the outside and back to place

 ALL DO SI DO YOUR PARTNERS
ALL DO SI DO YOUR CORNERS

 TAKE YOUR CORNER LADY
AND PROMENADE (to gents place)

SAME OLD GENT AND
HIS NEW YOUNG MATE

DOWN THE CENTER
THROUGH THE GOLDEN GATE

LADY GO RIGHT, (etc)
(each gent goes through the gate twice
repeat the above do si do calls.)

See page 24 to make a Complete Dance.

BIRDIE IN THE CAGE

FIRST COUPLE starts the dance

57

 LEAD TO THE RIGHT
Birdie in the center, three hands'round

 BIRDIE FLY OUT (lady)
HAWKIE FLY IN (gent)

HAWKIE FLY OUT
GIVE BIRDIE A SWING

FOUR HANDS AROUND

LEAD TO THE NEXT (etc)

Sometimes "The Birdie" who is the Lady, is called a hen and the gent, "The Hawk" is called a crow. Then when the Hen is in the center she "CACKLES" and the crow "CAWS". The person on the inside generally turns around in the opposite direction from that in which the three are going.

See page 26 to make a Complete Dance.

THE STAR

58

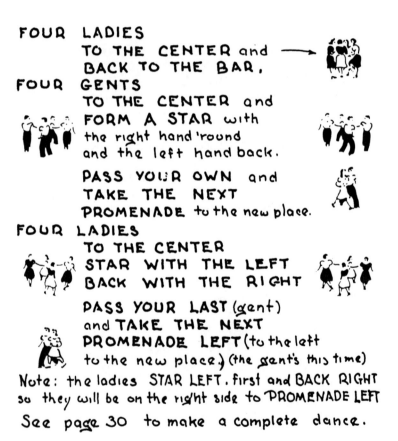

FOUR LADIES
   TO THE CENTER and →
   BACK TO THE BAR,
FOUR GENTS
   TO THE CENTER and
   FORM A STAR with
   the right hand 'round
   and the left hand back.

   PASS YOUR OWN and
   TAKE THE NEXT
   PROMENADE to the new place.
FOUR LADIES
   TO THE CENTER
   STAR WITH THE LEFT
   BACK WITH THE RIGHT

   PASS YOUR LAST (gent)
   and TAKE THE NEXT
   PROMENADE LEFT (to the left
   to the new place.) (the gent's this time)

Note: the ladies STAR LEFT. first and BACK RIGHT
so they will be on the right side to PROMENADE LEFT

See page 30 to make a complete dance.

SWING-O RING-O

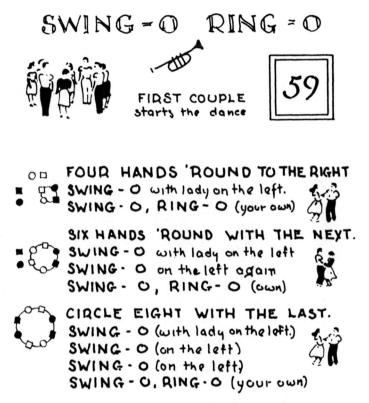

FIRST COUPLE
starts the dance

59

FOUR HANDS 'ROUND TO THE RIGHT
SWING - O with lady on the left.
SWING - O, RING - O (your own)

SIX HANDS 'ROUND WITH THE NEXT.
SWING - O with lady on the left
SWING - O on the left again
SWING - O, RING - O (own)

CIRCLE EIGHT WITH THE LAST.
SWING - O (with lady on the left.)
SWING - O (on the left)
SWING - O (on the left)
SWING - O, RING - O (your own)

This is a Version of BEACHCOMBER
46 It is just about the swingiest dance
going and should be danced only by
the robust or veteran — unless the beginner
needs taking down a peg.
See page 24 to make a Complete Dance.

DUCK AND DIVE

60 FIRST COUPLE starts the dance

 LEAD TO THE RIGHT
CIRCLE FOUR HALF WAY
DUCK AND DIVE

LEAD TO THE NEXT
RIGHT HANDS ACROSS
LEFT HANDS BACK

LEAD TO THE LAST
CIRCLE FOUR HALF WAY
DUCK AND DIVE

LEAD AWAY HOME and
EVERY BODY SWING

Combine these calls with calls from
page 32 as outlined on Page 26 to make a
complete dance.
Explanation of this dance on the following page

DUCK AND DIVE
Continued

CIRCLE FOUR HALF WAY - means to go around until the second couple is in the center between the 1st and 4th.

DUCK AND DIVE - the 1st couple then ducks under the raised hands of the 2nd. and continues on to the out side of the set where the 4th couple goes under them. The 1st couple then turns and goes back, under the 2nd, over the 4th. The 2nd and 4th couples follow the 1st. The couple on the outside always goes under the couple on the inside. It helps if the caller repeats **UNDER FROM THE OUTSIDE, UNDER FROM THE OUTSIDE** while the couples weave back and forth. Whenever a couple gets to the outside it immediately turns about and dives under the hands of the couple in the middle. When the first couple is back where it started from the call is **LEAD TO THE RIGHT** so they will stop diving otherwise they will just go on and on.

A good caller who is mathematically inclined can line the dancers up so that they can **DUCK AND DIVE** the length of the hall instead of just individual sets..

DOUBLE OR NOTHING

62	**2 HEAD COUPLES** Start the Dance.	

 LEAD TO THEIR RIGHT
CIRCLE FOUR AROUND

GENTS BACK TO PLACE

 SIDE GENTS RIGHT & LEFT
with the right hand lady.

BALANCE FOUR →
with the left hand lady

 TWO LONE GENTS BALANCE

SIDE GENTS' LADIES CHAIN
with the right hand lady

 DO SI DO FOUR
with the left hand lady

TWO LONE GENTS
LEAD TO THE RIGHT
CIRCLE FOUR

RIGHT AND LEFT EIGHT.

See page 28 to make a complete dance.

SHOP TALK

63

EIGHT HANDS 'ROUND the front office.
4 SECRETARIES - GRAND CHAIN
the office-force ALL DO SI DO
GRAND RIGHT AND LEFT

4 SALESMEN - GRAND CHAIN
the office-force ALL SWING
and ALL PROMENADE

4 SECRETARIES - STAR WITH RIGHT
BACK WITH THE LEFT.
the office-force ALL DO SI DO
GRAND RIGHT AND LEFT

4 SALESMEN - STAR WITH RIGHT
BACK WITH THE LEFT
the office-force ALL PROMENADE
right out to lunch.

This is a Complete Dance, but can be repeated.

CHASE THE SQUIRREL

64

FIRST COUPLE
starts the dance

#1

LEAD TO THE RIGHT
chase the squirrel 'round the two
LADY GOES 'ROUND and
GENT CUTS THROUGH

#2

Now back around the same old track
the **GENT GOES AROUND** and
the **LADY CUTS BACK** (back through)

CIRCLE FOUR

LEAD TO THE NEXT (etc.)

#1 First couple walks behind second couple
with, lady in the lead. Lady goes all the way
around, gent cuts between the standing two.
#2 This puts the gent in the lead. They
go around again. Gent goes all the way
around, lady cuts through. If the lady turns
and backs through she will be ready for
CIRCLE FOUR.

See page 26 to make a Complete Dance.

FIGURE EIGHT

FIRST LADY etc.
start the dance

65

[FIRST LADY AND OPPOSITE GENT]

AROUND WITH THE RIGHT
BACK WITH THE LEFT

right hand to partner
BALANCE 4 IN LINE

CUT A FIGURE EIGHT
WITH THE (first) GENT IN THE LEAD
Behind the fourth (couple) 'cross the
center, behind the second.

ALL   SWING.

This dance should be repeated for
each lady and her opposite gent.

See page 24 to make a complete dance.

HALF WAY HOUSE

66

2 HEAD LADIES
start the dance

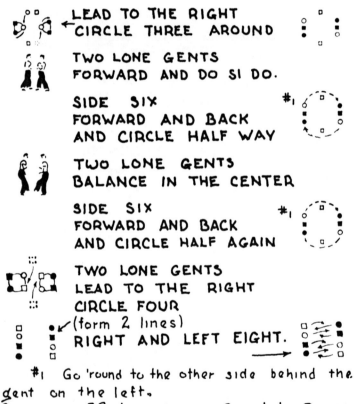

LEAD TO THE RIGHT
CIRCLE THREE AROUND

TWO LONE GENTS
FORWARD AND DO SI DO.

SIDE SIX
FORWARD AND BACK
AND CIRCLE HALF WAY

TWO LONE GENTS
BALANCE IN THE CENTER

SIDE SIX
FORWARD AND BACK
AND CIRCLE HALF AGAIN

TWO LONE GENTS
LEAD TO THE RIGHT
CIRCLE FOUR
(form 2 lines)
RIGHT AND LEFT EIGHT.

#1 Go 'round to the other side behind the
gent on the left.
See page 28 to make a Complete Dance.

BACHELORS' DELIGHT

ALL 4 GENTS
start the Dance

ALL FOUR GENTS

TO THE RIGHT of the ring
when you get there you
BALANCE AND SWING

when you get through
remember the call
ALLEMANDE LEFT AND
DROMENADE ALL ⟶

NOTE: gents PROMENADE with the lady they have swung each time and they always return to her place. It is only the gents who move around the □. The ladies return to their own places each time.

See page 30 to make a Complete Dance.

ON THE BEAM

68

2 HEAD COUPLES
start the Dance.

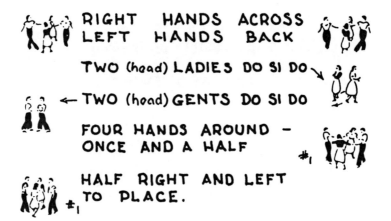

RIGHT HANDS ACROSS
LEFT HANDS BACK

TWO (head) LADIES DO SI DO

← TWO (head) GENTS DO SI DO

FOUR HANDS AROUND —
ONCE AND A HALF

#1

HALF RIGHT AND LEFT
TO PLACE.

#1

#1 When you get to the other side the second time in FOUR HANDS 'ROUND you walk through the opposite couple to your place in a HALF RIGHT AND LEFT.

See page 22 to make a Complete Dance.

THE TRADING POST

  **FIRST COUPLE** starts the dance

LEAD TO THE RIGHT
I'LL SWING YOUR GAL
YOU SWING MINE.

NOW YOU SWING YOUR GAL
I'LL SWING MINE

LADIES CHAIN, and
LEAD TO THE NEXT

Other ways of saying the above calls.
SWING YER OPPOSITE, SWING HER ALONE
SWING THE ONE YOU CALL YOUR OWN.
or
SWING YER OPPOSITE, DON'T BE AFRAID
SWING YOUR PARTNERS, AND PROMENADE
The calls can be used in the above order
each time a couple goes around the square
and the PROMENADE makes a fitting ending.
See page 26 to make a Complete Dance.

THE BASKET

70 | HEAD COUPLES start the Dance

FOUR HANDS AROUND

 CROSS EIGHT HANDS

LADIES BOW (so that gents can encircle them with joined hands)

 GENTS KNOW HOW (to bow - so that - ladies can encircle them with joined hands)

and AROUND YOU GO →
(to the left)

 LEFT HANDS BACK.

Combine these calls with calls from page 32 as outlined on page 28 to make a complete dance.

WHITE COLLAR GIRLS

2 HEAD LADIES
start the Dance

71

TURN YOUR RIGHT HAND GENT
WITH YOUR RIGHT HAND 'ROUND

 turn **OPPOSITE WITH THE LEFT**

 SWING YOUR PARTNER in the center

and **FOUR HANDS 'ROUND.**

This dance can be repeated or continued to include the gents or it can be called only for the gents.

See page 28 to make a Complete Dance.

INDIAN FILE

72

FIRST COUPLE
starts the dance

 LEAD TO THE RIGHT
FOUR HANDS AROUND.

THE OTHER WAY BACK, LADY IN THE
LEAD, SINGLE FILE, INDIAN STYLE

STOP AND SWING HER ONCE IN A WHILE.

 LEAD TO THE NEXT
SIX HANDS 'ROUND
(repeat "The Other Way" etc. twice)

LEAD TO THE LAST
EIGHT HANDS 'ROUND.
(repeat "The Other Way" etc three times)

See dances 46 and 59 for information on breaking the circle to include SIX and EIGHT. See page 24 to make a Complete Dance.

CASANOVA

73

EIGHT HANDS 'ROUND

HEADS	RIGHT AND LEFT
SIDES	RIGHT AND LEFT
ALL	PROMENADE WITH CORNER

HEADS	LADIES CHAIN
SIDES	LADIES CHAIN
ALL	PROMENADE WITH CORNER

HEADS	FOUR HANDS 'ROUND
SIDES	FOUR HANDS 'ROUND
ALL	PROMENADE WITH CORNER

HEADS	STAR WITH THE RIGHT
	BACK WITH THE LEFT
SIDES	STAR WITH THE RIGHT
	BACK WITH THE LEFT

ALL - PROMENADE
WITH YOUR OWN PARTNER

The Gents, each time, PROMENADE
with a new girl, to their own (gents) places.
It is the ladies who progress around the set.
This is a Complete Dance, but can be repeated.

VARIETY IN PATTERN #1

The pattern #1 type of dance does not necessarily have to follow the form on page 22. The different ways of dancing the same group of calls may be rotated or moved around to any position in the dance. Thus the first part (page 22) may be danced second or third. Also other ways of dancing it (as shown below) may be added.

The Dance

HEADS	FOUR HANDS AROUND
SIDES	RIGHT AND LEFT
HEADS	FORWARD AND BACK
SIDES	DO SI DO
SIDES	FOUR HANDS AROUND
HEADS	RIGHT AND LEFT
SIDES	FORWARD AND BACK
HEADS	DO SI DO

There is no reason (with experienced dancers) why the two head couples can't dance with the side couples on their right at the same time. That is, couple 1 dances with couple 2 while couple 3 dances with couple 4 and likewise couple 2 can dance with couple 3 while couple 4 dances with couple 1. Thus every couple dances with every other couple in the set and all couples can be dancing at the same time so there is no standing around.

Two Head Couples lead to their right

ALL FOUR HANDS AROUND
    RIGHT AND LEFT
    FORWARD AND BACK
    DO SI DO

ALL SWING YOUR PARTNERS, PROMENADE.

Two Side Couples lead to their right

ALL FOUR HANDS AROUND
    RIGHT AND LEFT
    FORWARD AND BACK
    DO SI DO

The Dance

An Ending

The Dance

An infinite number of dances can be arranged from even these few simple and basic dances. There are many more ideas and combinations that can be worked out. Everyone should get an equal amount of dancing no matter what variation is used. These variations should be danced only by experienced dancers.

VARIETY in PATTERN #3

The pattern #3 type of dance does not necessarily have to follow the form on page 26. Bits of "Pattern #1" can be added to these dances to make them longer and more interesting. Also if the two head couples lead to the side couples on their right as in "Pattern #1 Variety" these two types of dances can be mixed together into one dance as illustrated below.

An Opening
The Dance

ALL EIGHT HANDS AROUND
    HEADS FOUR HANDS AROUND
    SIDES FOUR HANDS AROUND
    HEADS RIGHT AND LEFT
    SIDES RIGHT AND LEFT
    HEADS FORWARD AND BACK
    SIDES FORWARD AND BACK
    HEADS DO SI DO
    SIDES DO SI DO

An Ending
The Dance

ALL SWING YOUR PARTNERS, PROMENADE.
TWO HEAD COUPLES
    LEAD TO THEIR RIGHT, FOUR HANDS 'ROUND
    DIP FOR THE OYSTER, DIG FOR THE CLAM

DIVE FOR THE SARDINE, GET A FULL CAN.

An Ending

The Dance

ALL-SWING YOUR PARTNER, PROMENADE

HEADS FOUR HANDS AROUND
SIDES RIGHT AND LEFT
HEADS FORWARD AND BACK
SIDES DO SI DO
SIDES FOUR HANDS AROUND
HEADS RIGHT AND LEFT
SIDES FORWARD AND BACK
HEADS DO SI DO

ALL-SWING YOUR PARTNERS, PROMENADE.

An Ending

TWO SIDE COUPLES

LEAD TO THEIR RIGHT, FOUR HANDS 'ROUND
DIP FOR THE OYSTER, DIG FOR THE CLAM
DIVE FOR THE SARDINE, GET A FULL CAN.

The Dance

ALL-SWING YOUR PARTNERS, PROMENADE.

An Ending

The combining of dances should be very carefully worked out. Everyone should get an equal amount of dancing no matter what variation is used. The fundamentals must be understood and mastered before any fancy combinations are attempted.

THE NINE PIN

78 The nine pin, an extra, lady or gent, stands in the center of the set.

The object is for the nine pin to get a partner when the other dancers change partners. Regular endings from page 32 should be mixed in and the whole repeated to make the dance longer.

EIGHT HANDS AROUND THE NINE PIN, NINE HANDS AROUND.

 RIGHT HAND TO PARTNER GRAND RIGHT AND LEFT.

 ALL SWING NEW PARTNERS & PROMENADE (nine pin tries to get a partner)

(If the nine pin is a gent)

THE FOUR GENTS FOUR HANDS AROUND THE NINE PIN

 NOW THE FOUR LADIES FOUR HANDS AROUND THE NINE PIN (If the nine pin is a lady reverse last two calls)

ALL FORWARD AND SWING NEW PARTNERS (nine pin tries to get a partner) and **PROMENADE.**

8 HANDS AROUND THE 9 PIN ALL SWING YOUR OPPOSITE (nine pin tries to get a partner)

This is the Procedure

The circle dance is a natural departure from the square dance and will follow with little effort. There are no special opening calls for the circle dance. The dance is simply a series of calls, repeated over and over again. These calls are the same as the ones danced in the square dance, so the only new thing to learn is the manner in which the dancers progress around the circle.

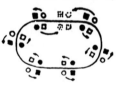
"The Circle" is danced by small groups arranged around the hall in a large circle. These groups consist of 4, 6, or 8 people. After dancing one complete set of changes, the group divides, each half progresses around the circle, in the direction it is facing, and repeats the complete set of calls with every other group in turn.

When the dancers again meet the other half of their original group, or when the dance has been done long enough the circle dance is generally ended by the call:—

ALL JOIN HANDS in one large circle.
GRAND RIGHT AND LEFT.
ALL SWING your partners
and PROMENADE
you know where and I don't care.

SICILIAN CIRCLE

 80 4 people in a Set
Circle Formation

 FOUR HANDS AROUND

 **RIGHT AND LEFT**

LADIES CHAIN

 PASS THROUGH (to next group)

Repeat calls until original dancers
meet again or as long as desired.

SOLDIER'S JOY

 4 people in a Set
Circle Formation

(81)

 FOUR HANDS 'ROUND

 SWING YOUR OPPOSITE

FOUR HANDS 'ROUND [1]

 SWING YOUR OWN

LADIES CHAIN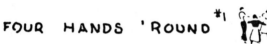

 FORWARD and **PASS THROUGH**
(to next group)

[1] This is often danced with out the second four hands around.
Repeat calls until original dancers meet again or as long as desired.

SCOTCH REEL

82

4 People in a Set
Circle Formation

 turn your **OPPOSITE WITH THE RIGHT**

turn your **PARTNER WITH THE LEFT**

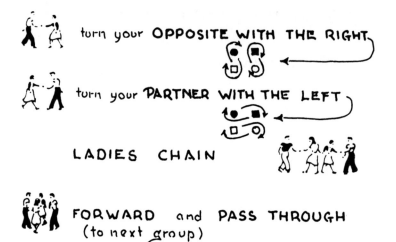

LADIES   CHAIN

FORWARD and **PASS THROUGH**
(to next group)

Repeat calls until original dancers
meet again or as long as desired.

TWO TO ONE

 6 People in a Set
Circle Formation

83

 SIX HANDS AROUND

 SWING ON THE RIGHT
(swing the opposite lady on the right)

 LADIES CHAIN
with right hand partner

 THREE HANDS AROUND with own

 FORWARD and **PASS THROUGH**
(to next group)

Note: When the dance is half over, everyone should face about the other way, right where they stand. This allows the ladies to get an equal share of swinging etc. (called by caller)

Repeat calls until original dancers meet again or as long as desired.

FIFTH COLUMN REEL

84

6 People in a Set
Circle Formation

SIX HANDS AROUND

RIGHT AND LEFT
(with the right hand lady)

SWING (with left hand lady)

THREE HANDS AROUND
(with both ladies)

#1

**ALL FORWARD AND BACK
WITH THE RIGHT HAND OVER
AND THE LEFT HAND UNDER.**

PASS THROUGH (to next group)

#1   The underhanded movement. — the 2
ladies change to the other side of the gent
while holding the gent's hands. The lady on
the left goes under the joined hands of the
gent and the other lady.

Repeat calls until original dancers
meet again or as long as desired.

PORTLAND FANCY

8 People in a Set
Circle Formation

85

EIGHT HANDS AROUND

RIGHT AND LEFT

LADIES CHAIN

ALL FORWARD AND BACK

FORWARD AGAIN and
PASS THROUGH

Repeat calls until original dancers
meet again or as long as desired.

WEST COAST REEL

86

8 People in a Set
Circle Formation

 EIGHT HANDS AROUND

 OUTSIDE couple balance and **SWING**
INSIDE couple **RIGHT AND LEFT**

OUTSIDE couple **RIGHT AND LEFT**
INSIDE couple balance and **SWING**

ALL LADIES CHAIN

ALL FORWARD and **PASS THROUGH**
(to the next group)

Repeat calls until original dancers
meet again or as long as desired.

This is the Procedure

A set consists of six couples in two contrary lines; all the gents in one line on the right and all the ladies in the opposite line facing them. The idea of the dance is to have the 1, 3, 5, couples progress toward the foot of the set while the other couples work toward the head.

The calls are meant for couples 1, 3, 5 who generally start the dance and continue dancing until they reach the foot. The even numbered dancers 2, 4, 6 thus naturally move toward the top (or head). Those who reach the top, cross over if the dance calls for it: that is, the lady and gent change places at the head. Then as soon as the couple below is free for them to dance with, the new head couple dances the same set of calls until it reaches the foot. There this couple waits one dance, and crosses back if it crossed over to begin with. As soon as another couple comes along for them to dance with, this couple progresses up the line again.

There are no special opening calls for the Contra dance. The dance calls are repeated over and over again for each new couple. When the dancers return to their original places, the dance ends with the call –

ALL FORWARD AND SWING your partners.

88   Here are the Contra Calls

Note: most of the calls on pages 15 to 20 apply to Contras as well as the Squares and Circles.

DOWN THE OUTSIDE and back.

Walk down the outside of the line that you are in toward the foot and come back to place.

DOWN THE CENTER and back.

Walk down the center of the set with your partner, turn at the foot, and walk back again on the same side of the set to your place. Do not walk too far; four steps are plenty.

CAST OFF

 This is always preceded by "Down the Center and Back" It means to move one position down the line. As you come BACK, you walk through your old place, go behind the person next below you in line, and come out below him so that he moves up the line as you move down it. "Cast Off" is really done by putting your arm behind the person next below you who pivots in his own place.

THE ONE BELOW

The one in line beside you who is nearer the foot of the set.

OREGON TRAIL

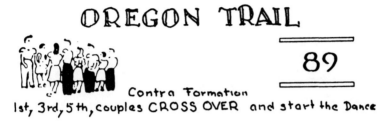

Contra Formation

1st, 3rd, 5th, couples CROSS OVER and start the Dance

SWING THE ONE BELOW

LADIES CHAIN

 FOUR HANDS AROUND

ALL FORWARD AND BACK

This is about the easiest Contra Dance there is. It is good to show the dancers the way to work up and down the line.

Repeat until couples return to original positions

LADY OF THE LAKE

90

Contra Formation

1st, 3rd, 5th couples CROSS OVER and start the Dance.

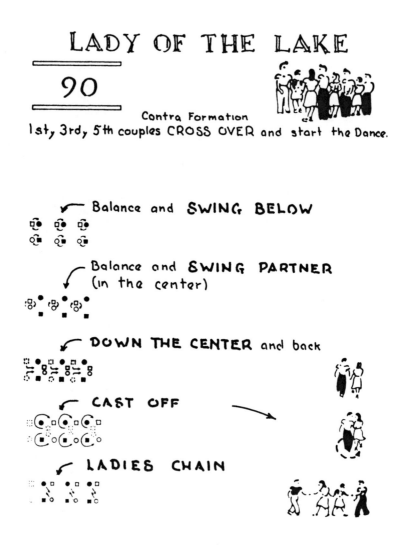

Balance and **SWING BELOW**

Balance and **SWING PARTNER**
(in the center)

DOWN THE CENTER and back

CAST OFF

LADIES CHAIN

Repeat until couples return to original positions

LADY WALPOLE'S REEL

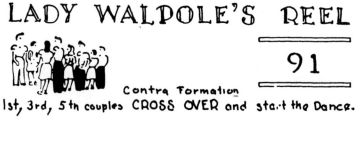

91

Contra Formation

1st, 3rd, 5th couples CROSS OVER and start the Dance.

SWING the one BELOW

 DOWN THE CENTER and back

CAST OFF

LADIES CHAIN

 PROMENADE HALF and

HALF RIGHT AND LEFT

This is probably the most pleasing of the simpler old time contras.

Repeat until couples return to original positions.

MORNING STAR

92

Contra Formation

1st, 3rd, 5th couples start the Dance.

RIGHT HAND TO PARTNER
BALANCE AND SWING

LEFT HAND TO PARTNER
BALANCE AND SWING

DOWN THE CENTER and back

CAST OFF

RIGHT AND LEFT

Repeat until couples return to original positions.

VIRGINIA REEL

Originally danced only by head lady and foot gent alternating with head gent and foot lady.

ALL

FORWARD AND BACK

turn with the **RIGHT HAND**

turn with the **LEFT HAND**

turn with **BOTH HANDS**

BACK TO BACK (do si do)

HEAD COUPLE

Right arm to partner and **REEL**

The head couple elbow swing in the center then around with each couple in turn (gent with ladies, lady with gents) each time alternating with Partner in the center.

Head couple **UP THE CENTER** and **MARCH** around and down the outside, up the center to place with every one following Then just the Head Couple down the center to become the foot Couple.

Repeat until couples return to original positions.

Many callers use this to change the dancer's
spirit from ballroom dancing to country dancing.

This is a transition dance. It
is used to give the dancers the
country dance spirit.   It is a
couple dance that can include waltzes
polkas, fox trots, etc.   The idea is to mix
the crowd. The more partners each dancer gets, the better.

The dance can start with a waltz
(or fox trot, etc).   When the couples are
all dancing the call is .....

ALL FORM A LARGE CIRCLE.
(ladies to the right of their gents)
RIGHT HAND TO YOUR PARTNER
GRAND RIGHT AND LEFT.
ALL DANCE with the one in front
of you.

This call may be varied by calling for
two circles, ladies in the center one.
Ladies go to the right, gents to the
left, then each dances with the one in
front of him.   Or, all the ladies at one
end of the hall, all the gents at the
other.   Then the gents (or the ladies)
go down and pick out a partner. The last
version is a good one to end this with, since
original partners can get together again.
There are many other ideas that also can
be used.

TIPS IN GENERAL

As a help to new callers who have never heard a dance called, there are many phonograph records with callings on them. It might be well to listen to three or four and develop a style of your own. The calls should be very clear and distinct so that beginners will understand every thing you are saying. The reason Old Timers could sacrifice clearness for the fun of singing and rhyming was that the dancers knew every step in the dance which never varied. ♉ The dance never starts until all the sets are complete, and each couple that wants to dance is in a set. ♉ The calls do not have to be followed word for word. A good caller can make up his own wording and rhymes, and that is his privilege just as long as the dancers can understand him. ♉ At the beginning of all dances, the caller should pick a certain couple to watch throughout the dance, so that he will always know just how far the dance has progressed. ♉ The caller must keep order at all times if he wants to keep group-interest in this type of dancing. ♉ The caller should impress upon his beginners that the calls are the simplest, most natural way of explaining the movements. A beginner can complicate them if he tends to doubt his first quick impulse. ♉ For groups of 32 people or more it is better for the caller to have an amplifier. Then he can talk into the microphone, concentrate on the dance, and not worry about making his voice heard.

96 A universal ending call for the last dance in a set of squares, as well as the circles and contras is : **ALL SWING YOUR PARTNERS AND PROMENADE - YOU KNOW WHERE AND I DON'T CARE** . (Meaning this dance is over, I don't care where you go now.)

TIPS ON THE SQUARE DANCE

In teaching the square dance, first form the square and teach the names of the positions. Then select a dance (pattern #1) and have the dancers walk through each of the calls in that dance as explained in detail under "Here are the Calls" (pp. 15 - 20) until each person knows just what to do when he hears that call. Next, select a simple closing from the group listed under "Openings and Endings" such as "SWING YOUR PARTNERS and PROMENADE. After the dancers get the idea pick a simple opening from the same page such as **EIGHT HANDS AROUND** and the dance is on. ⚹ After the first few dances it will probably be necessary to have only the first couple of each set walk through the new changes, as they are said and explained in order to have all the dancers understand them. ⚹ The caller must memorize at least one "Opening and Ending" call from page 32 and eventually all of them, as well as the general outline or "Pattern" of the different types of square dances. Then with the book open to the particular square selected, the caller may call the changes on that page, inserting simple

endings according to the proper memor- **97**
ized pattern. The first few times it might be well
for the Amateur caller to use the calls in the different
patterns, word for word. ℞ The simplified technique, as
used in this book, was developed for the benifit of the caller
as well as the dancer. The caller does not have to learn
the square dance tunes by heart or know exactly with
which measures the different calls should go. The
natural rhythm of the music will dictate to a large
extent the time it takes the dancers to complete a call,
so the caller should judge this time and call the next
call just a second before the dancers are ready for it.
℞ After the dancers and the caller have become
experienced, the caller may take a single tune for
a certain "dance", and, filling in around the
calls with his own rhymings, have a dance
that will correspond with the old-timers' "Singing
Calls". The old timers, who danced all their
lives in one or two towns, considered this
specialization ideal. But with the development
of present day travel the dances should be ver
satile enough to satisfy dancers from all localities.
℞ A good caller watches the dancers, judges
the timing and calls the next change as soon as
possible, just before they are ready for it, so
there is no waiting for the call. A good example
of this is in the type #1 Pattern which alternates
Heads and Sides.. In the call LADIES CHAIN
the call should immeadiately be SIDES as soon as
the head ladies start back for their own places,
then the side ladies can be crossing while the
head ladies are being turned by their partners.

98 An individual set should not rush ahead just because it knows the dance, but rather should wait for the caller to call the changes. The fun of the dance is in all doing it together in regular time. ✠ If faster individual sets insist on showing off by going on ahead of the calls and the general group, the caller can really <u>show them up</u> by adding or inserting different and extra changes. ✠ Every caller should have on the tip of his tongue a simple ending such as "<u>All Swing Your Partners & Promenade</u>". Then he will never be caught napping, for he can always call that and think hard of what comes next. ✠ To get the dancers on the floor, the band usually plays a little square dance music so the dancers get the spirit of the thing then the call is — ALL CHOOSE PARTNERS FOR A PLAIN QUADRILLE, (or the name of one square dance) This can be followed by FOUR COUPLES AROUND A SQUARE. To add color, the calls of the dance can be repeated while the sets are forming.

TIPS ON THE CIRCLE DANCE

The circle dance offers no special problems to the caller. One individual group can not get ahead of the others because it cannot dance with the next group until that group finishes dancing with the last one. ✠ To get the dancers on the floor the band usually plays a little square dance music so that the dancers get the spirit of the dance,

Then the call is — ALL CHOOSE YOUR
PARTNERS FOR (name of circle dance.)
A CIRCLE OF SETS AROUND THE HALL.
To add color, the calls of the dance can be
repeated while the dancers are forming the
circle. ✠ The calls in a type #1 pattern square
dance may be used as a series of calls for
a circle dance if the call PASS-THROUGH is
added. ✠ The call FORWARD AND BACK which
generally precedes the call "Pass-Through" is
used as an equalizer. The faster groups dance
it, while the slower groups leave it out so that
they all may pass through together. ✠ If the dancers
are warned, the routine of the circle dance may
be changed during the dance to add interest
and variety. This should be done only with experienced groups and it should not be changed
more than once or twice.

TIPS ON THE CONTRA DANCE

To the beginner who has never seen
or danced a contra dance it is the
hardest type of the three to under
stand.. The easiest way for a caller to teach
the contras is to have the head couple, only,
start the dance. First, be sure that all the gents
are in the right hand line and all the ladies in the
left, even in the dances that say to cross over.
Then if the dance does say to cross
over, have the head couple.only, cross
over. As the head couple starts dancing
with the third couple, the second couple becomes

100 the new head and does the same things as the first couple, ... dancing with each couple in turn. If the dancers crossed over at the head they must be sure to cross back at the foot. By starting only one couple at a time the caller or instructor can help each couple as it begins at the head. This is the way the contras were meant to be danced originally but after everyone knows how to do the dance it is better to have the 1st, 3rd, and 5th couples begin the dance. It will make the dance shorter and everyone can start dancing much sooner. ¶ Every other time the calls are repeated, that is, every time a new head couple is ready to start dancing, the caller adds the call ON THE HEAD or AT THE HEAD. ¶ More than 6 couples may dance in a set but this is a long slow type of dance and each couple added at the end of the line makes the dance just that much longer. ¶ The routine of a contra dance should NOT be changed during a dance. New dances can be made but the routine is so short and is repeated so many times that any change would discourage the dancers and spoil the dance. ¶ To get the dancers on the floor, the band usually plays a little music; then the call is ALL CHOOSE YOUR PARTNERS FOR (name of the contra dance) SIX COUPLES IN A SET, ALL THE GENTS ON THE RIGHT, ALL THE LADIES ON THE LEFT. To add color, the calls of the dance may be repeated while the sets are forming.

"Swing Your Partners" was written to make the pattern and procedure of the country dances clear to the beginner. When he has mastered the fundamentals he may want to know about the Background and History of this type of dancing, as well as to add the more complicated dances to his list. The following books will help him:

DICK'S QUADRILLE CALL-BOOK   1878-1923
     FITZGERALD PUBLISHING CORP.   NEW YORK.

PROMPTING, JOHN M. SCHELL   1890
     CARL FISCHER, INC., NEW YORK

PROMPTER'S HAND BOOK, FRENCH   1893
     OLIVER DITSON CO.   BOSTON

OLD SQUARE DANCES OF AMERICA, BOYD. 1925
     H.T. FITZ SIMONS CO.   CHICAGO

GOOD MORNING,   HENRY FORD   1926
     DEARBORN PUBLISHING Co. DEARBORN, MICH.

DANCES OF OUR PIONEERS, RYAN   1926-1939
     A.S. BARNES & CO. NEW YORK

THE COUNTRY DANCE BOOK - TOLMAN & PAGE 1937
     THE COUNTRYMAN PRESS, GUILFORD, VT,

COWBOY DANCES,   SHAW   1939
     THE CAXTON PRINTERS, LTD., CALDWELL, IDAHO

Printed in the United Stat
134822LV00015B/139/A

9 781430 447481